Make It Spooky

Freaky Food for Halloween

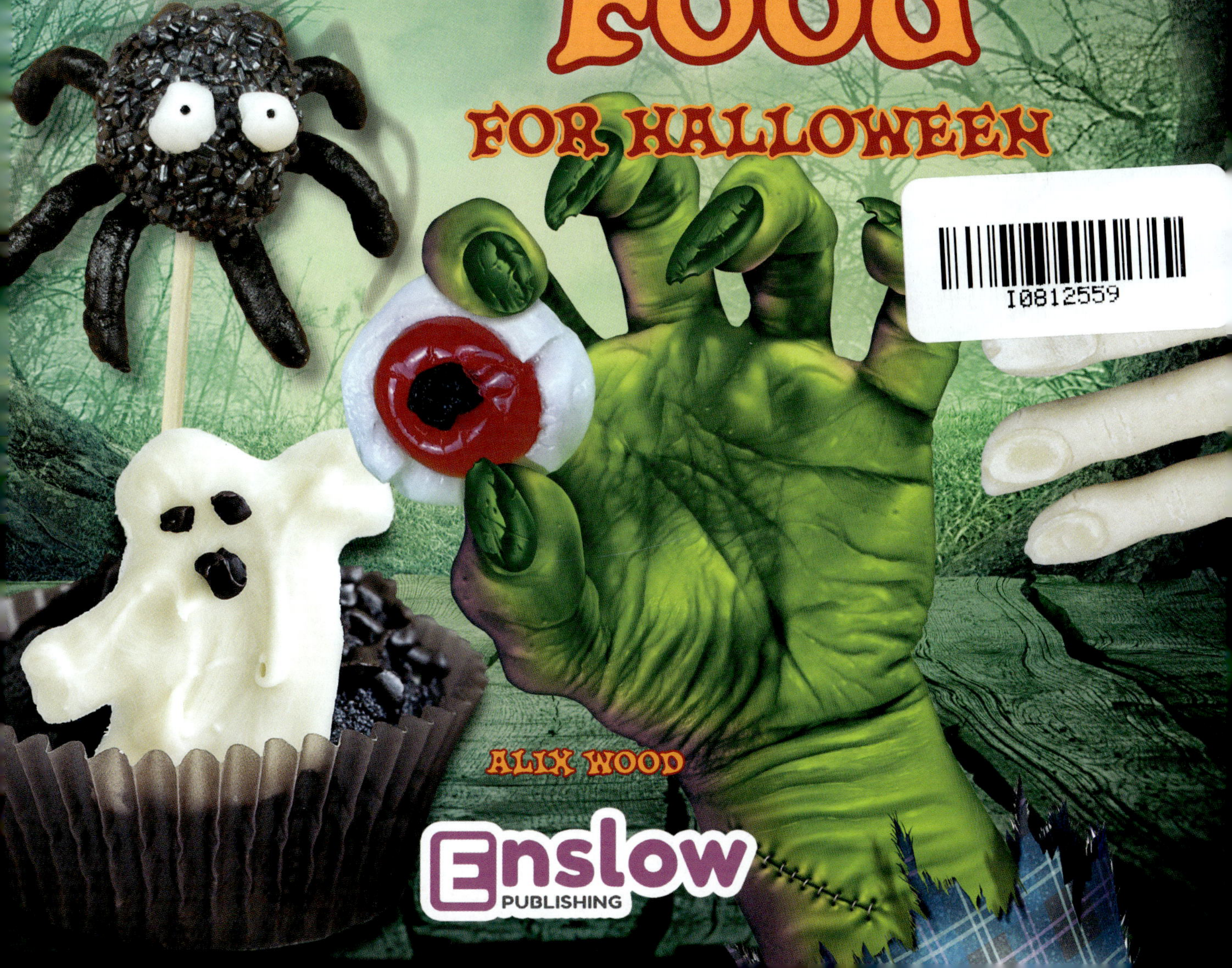

Alix Wood

Enslow Publishing

Published in 2023 by Enslow Publishing, LLC
29 East 21st Street, New York, NY 10010

Written and designed by Alix Wood
Projects devised by Kevin Wood

Cataloging-in-Publication Data

Names: Wood, Alix.
Title: Freaky food for Halloween / Alix Wood.
Description: New York : Enslow Publishing, 2023. | Series: Make it spooky | Includes glossary and index.
Identifiers: ISBN 9781978531222 (pbk.) | ISBN 9781978531246 (library bound) | ISBN 9781978531239 (6pack) | ISBN 9781978531253 (ebook)
Subjects: LCSH: Halloween cooking--Juvenile literature.
Classification: LCC TX739.2.H34 W64 2023 | DDC 641.5'68--dc23

Manufactured in the United States of America

CPSIA compliance information: Batch #CSENS23: For further information contact
Enslow Publishing LLC, New York, New York at 1-800-398-2504.

Contents

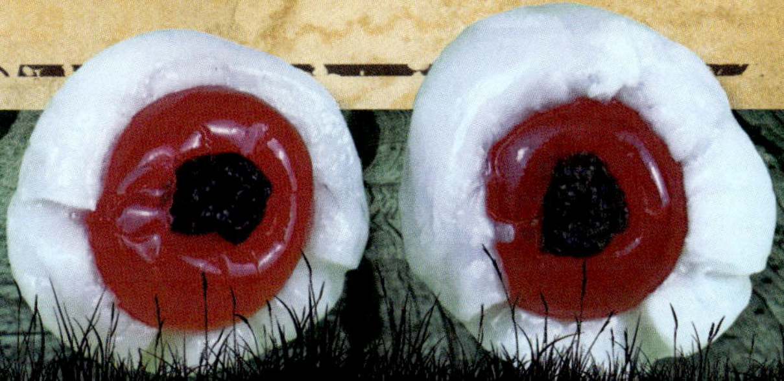

Spooky Food

This book tells you everything you need to make truly disgusting-looking snacks! They may look gross, but amazingly, they all taste really good.

You Will Need

Each project has a list of ingredients you will need. You also need some everyday kitchen items such as bowls, spoons, a knife, and serving dishes.

TIP

Tomato sauce makes great blood spatters for savory food. For sweet food, try some red fruit jelly, or try the fruit sauce from page 13.

Adult Help

When you see this symbol you may need a little adult help. It usually means something needs to be heated up or cut with a knife.

Make It Super-Spooky

Make Edible Mud!

You Will Need

- 1 package dark chocolate cookies
- a ziplock food bag
- a rolling pin

Why not serve your food on plates of mud? It's easy to make and tastes surprisingly delicious!

1

If your cookies have a cream filling, twist the cookies to open them. Scrape the filling off using a blunt knife.

2

Put the cookies in the ziplock bag. Seal the bag shut. Crush the cookies into small pieces using the rolling pin.

3

The jello worms on page 22 look great served in mud!

Maggot Balls

You Will Need

- 4 tablespoons butter
- 1 bag mini-marshmallows
- 2 tablespoons corn syrup
- 1/2 teaspoon clear vanilla
- 5 cups puffed rice cereal
- vegetable oil
- wax paper
- clean flower pot

1

Adult Help

Ask an adult to help you melt the butter in a large saucepan over low heat.

2

Add the marshmallows to the butter. Stir them until they begin to melt. Then add the corn syrup.

3

Keep stirring the mixture until the marshmallows are almost all melted.

4

Take the pan off the heat. Stir in the vanilla. Then stir in the puffed rice cereal.

5

Let the mixture cool. Put a few drops of vegetable oil on your hands. Roll handfuls of the mixture into balls.

TIP

Rolling the maggot balls can get messy. Wearing rubber gloves helps keep your hands from getting sticky.

6

Line a baking sheet with wax paper. Put the balls on the tray. Leave them to set for a few hours. Serve the balls in a clean flower pot.

Frozen Ghosts

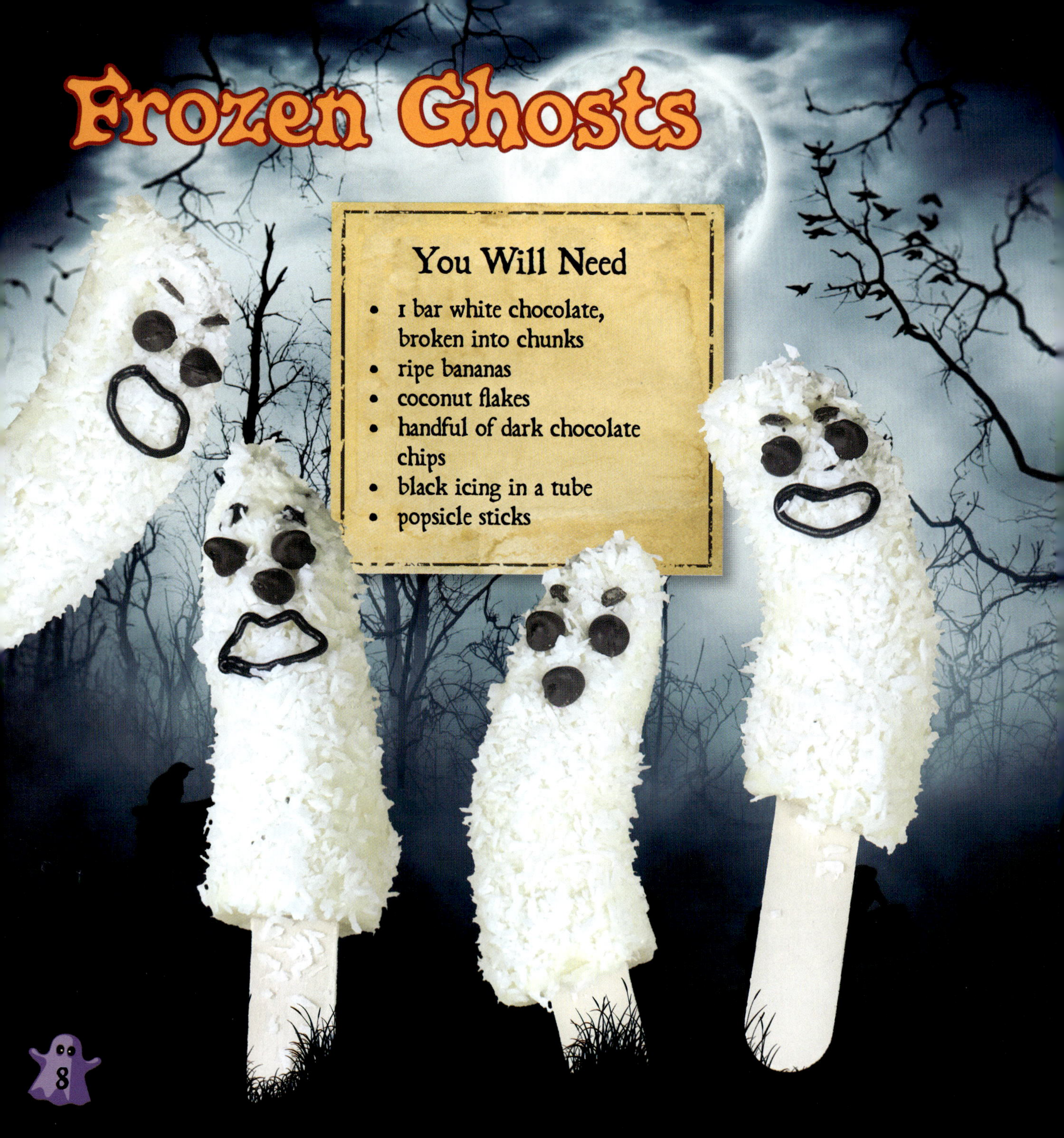

You Will Need

- 1 bar white chocolate, broken into chunks
- ripe bananas
- coconut flakes
- handful of dark chocolate chips
- black icing in a tube
- popsicle sticks

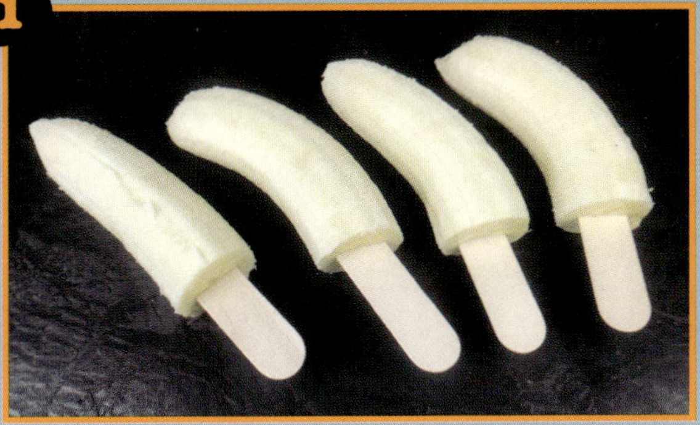

1

Peel the bananas. Cut them in half. Then push a popsicle stick into the cut end of each piece of banana.

2

Adult Help

Put the white chocolate chunks into a heatproof bowl. Ask an adult to place the bowl over a pan of simmering water. Slowly melt the chocolate, then let it cool.

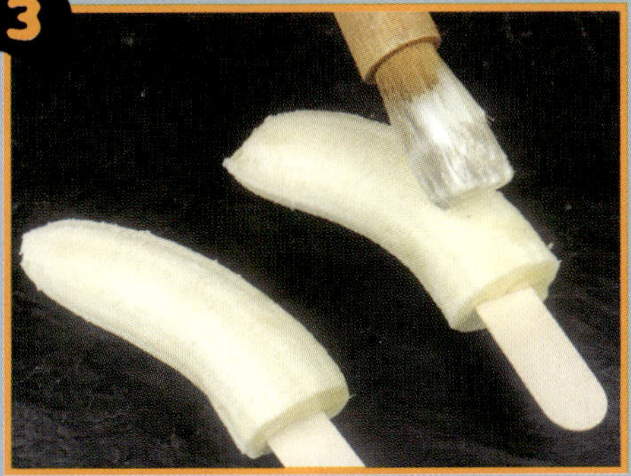

3

Using a pastry brush, coat the bananas in the melted white chocolate.

4

Sprinkle the bananas with coconut. Put them on a tray lined with wax paper. Make the faces using chocolate chips and icing. Put them in the freezer for around four hours.

Frightening Fruit

You Will Need

- satsuma or clementine oranges
- 1 stick celery
- 1 larger orange
- other small fruit pieces
- a pumpkin cutter or knife

1 Adult Help

Ask an adult to help you cut the top off an orange.

2

Scoop out inside of the orange using a spoon.

3 Adult Help

Use a pumpkin cutter, or ask an adult to help you cut a pumpkin face into the orange skin using a knife.

4

Fill your pumpkin orange with fruit.

5

Peel the satsumas or clementines completely.

6

Adult Help

Ask an adult to help you cut a stick of celery into smaller sticks.

7

Poke a celery stick into the hole at the top of each fruit pumpkin.

TIP

You could put the insides and juice of the orange into the punch on page 30.

Pear Ghouls

You Will Need

- a few pears
- 1 walnut
- sprinkles
- handful of raspberries and blackberries
- a few blueberries
- two tablespoons sugar
- a potato peeler
- a jug, saucepan, sieve, and spoon

1 Adult Help

Heat the berries and sugar in a saucepan.

2

Press the berry mixture through a sieve into a jug.

3 Adult Help

Ask an adult to help peel the pears and dig out holes for the eyes and mouth using a potato peeler. Cut the top off one pear.

4

Spoon the berry sauce into each eye and into the mouth.

5

Put some sauce and a walnut brain on the cut pear. Decorate with blueberry eyes and sprinkles for the mouth.

TIP

Make your ghouls even more gruesome by dripping some blood-red sauce on their serving dish.

Eyeball Jello

You Will Need

- 1 can lychees in syrup
- cocktail cherries
- raisins
- strawberry or raspberry jello

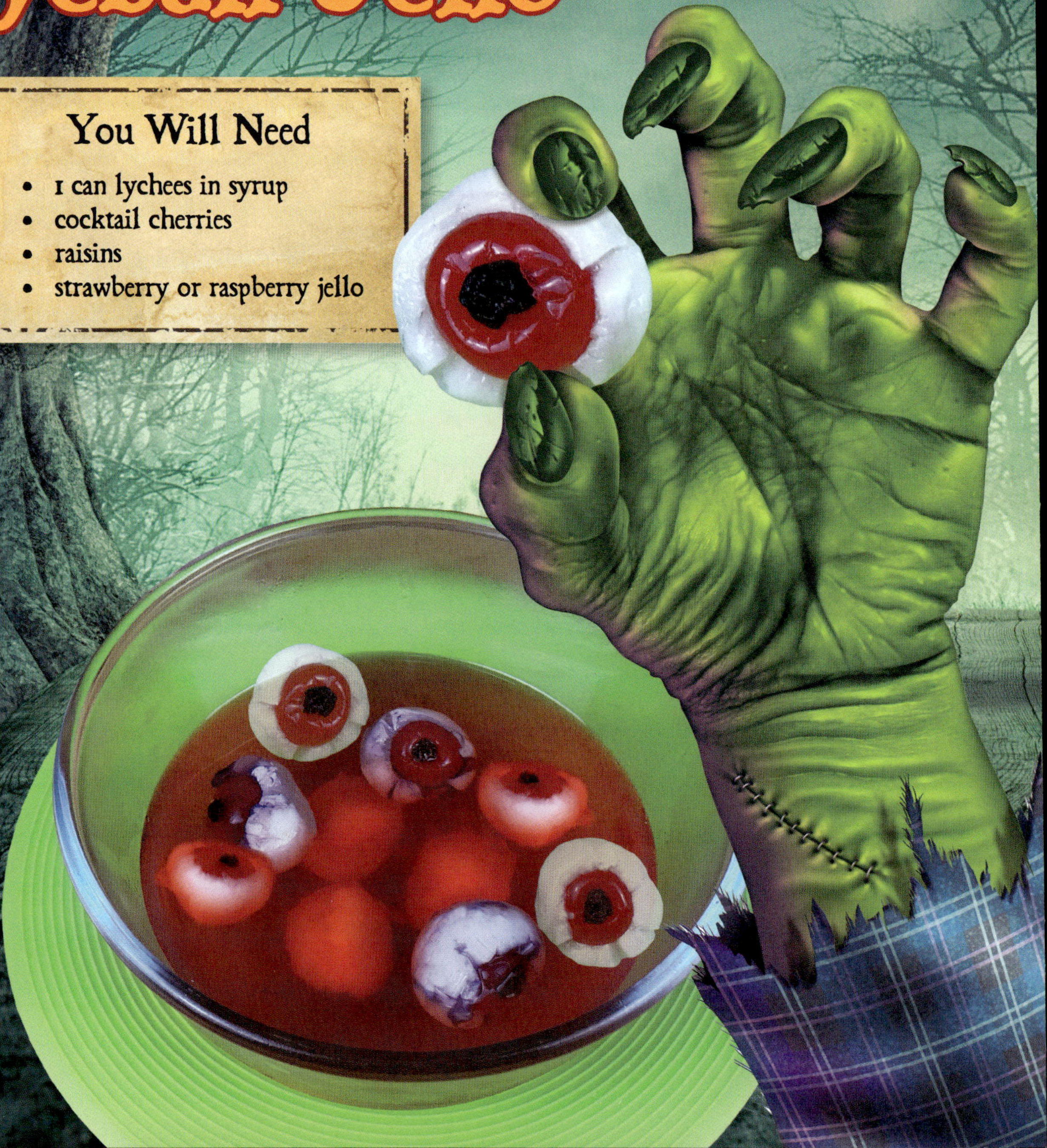

1 Adult Help

Ask an adult to help you open the tin of lychees. Drain off the syrup. You could use it in the water when you make the jello.

2 Adult Help

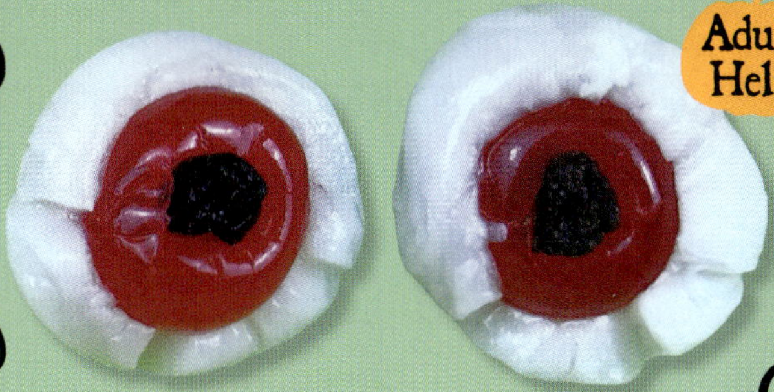

Put a cherry inside each lychee, in the hole made when they removed the stone. If your lychees still have stones in them, ask an adult to help remove them. Then push a raisin into each cherry.

3

Make the jello according to the package instructions.

4

Pour half the jello into a glass bowl. Add some eyeballs. Place in the fridge to set.

5

Once set, place more eyeballs on the top. Pour more jello over them. Put the bowl back in the fridge. Repeat this step once more.

TIP

It looks really spooky if your eyeballs peer out of the bowl in all directions.

Wormy Peppers

You Will Need

- orange bell peppers
- canned spaghetti
- a baking sheet
- a pumpkin cutter or knife
- a toothpick

TIP

When you dish up your pepper, scatter some spaghetti around the outside to make it look as if the worms are crawling away.

1

With an adult's help, cut the top off an orange bell pepper. Set the top aside. Scrape the seeds out of the middle of the pepper and throw them away.

2

Draw a pumpkin face on the pepper by pressing into the skin with a toothpick. Cut out your design using a pumpkin cutter, or ask an adult for help using a knife.

3

Spoon some spaghetti into the pepper. Put the top back on and bake the pepper in a medium oven for around half an hour.

4

Your pumpkin pepper looks super spooky if some spaghetti pokes out of the eye holes!

Finger Buffet

Sausage Fingers

You Will Need

- sausages or hot dogs
- tomato ketchup
- hot dog buns
- a blunt knife

1

Cut your sausages into finger-sized. pieces. We cut these large ones in half.

2

With a blunt knife, make a shallow cut near the end of the sausage. Turn the knife so it is flat. Cut away half an inch from the top of the sausage.

3

Adult Help

Make a few little cuts across each sausage for the knuckles. Ask an adult for help cooking the sausages.

4

Squirt gruesome ketchup over your sausage fingers.

Sweet Fingers

You Will Need

- marzipan or cookie dough
- almonds
- a tube of red frosting
- a blunt knife

1

Shape some marzipan to look like fingers. Press an almond into the end of each finger.

2

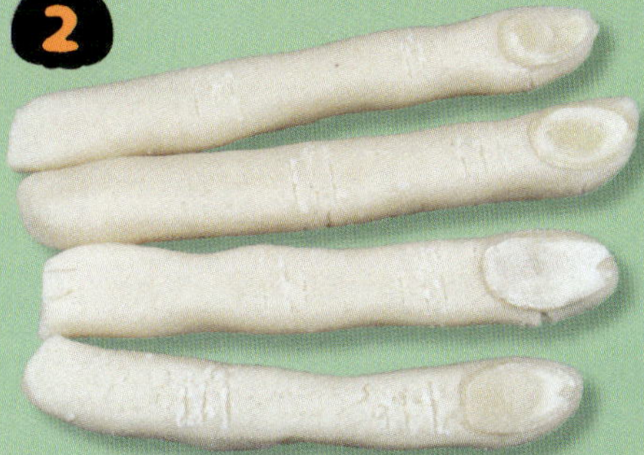

Adult Help

To make the knuckles, make a few cuts with a blunt knife. If you're using cookie dough, ask an adult to help you bake the cookies at this point.

3

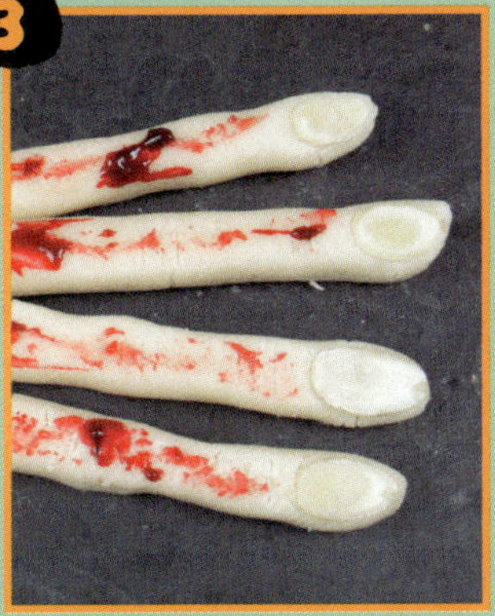

Squeeze a tube of red frosting onto your marzipan or baked cookie fingers.

You could bury your creepy fingers in the edible mud you made on page 5.

Cake Pop Spiders

You Will Need

- dark chocolate
- some cake pops
- black chocolate sandwich cookies or black sprinkles
- wooden skewers
- 1 tube of white icing
- licorice sticks or rope
- long toothpicks

1

Adult Help

Ask an adult to help you break the chocolate into pieces and heat them gently in a bowl over a pan of hot water.

TIP

If you don't have any cake pops, carve a cupcake or a piece of sponge cake into a ball using a blunt knife.

2

Using a long toothpick, dip the cake pop into the melted chocolate.

3

If you are using cookies, crush them up. Put the crumbs or sprinkles in a bowl.

4

Dip the chocolate-covered cake pop into the crumbs or sprinkles.

5

Cut four pieces of licorice to fit the cake pop. Cross them to create eight legs.

6

Squeeze some eyeballs onto the spider using a tube of white icing.

7

Pierce through the legs and then the body with the skewer. Press a black crumb onto each eye.

Jello Worms

You Will Need

- package of raspberry or strawberry jello
- some straws
- a tall, thin container small enough to hold the straws snugly

1

Bunch together a handful of straws.

2

Find a narrow container that is taller than the straws. The straws must fit the container snugly. We used a tall vase.

3

Make the jello following the package instructions, but only add half the cold water.

TIP
If you want brown worms, add some green food coloring to the water.

4

Let the jello cool a little. Pour it into the container, but not right to the top.

5

Lower the straws into the jello. You should see the straws fill up with jello.

6

If necessary, add more jello to cover the straws.
If the straws rise over the edge, add more straws to wedge them. Put in the refrigerator for 2-3 hours.

7

To squeeze out your jello worms, press along the straw with your thumb and forefinger.

Edible Ghosts

You Will Need

- some cupcakes
- ready-to-roll white fondant icing
- chocolate chips
- a squeezy tube of icing
- popsicle sticks
- a blunt knife

1

Cut some ready-to-roll fondant into a circle.

2

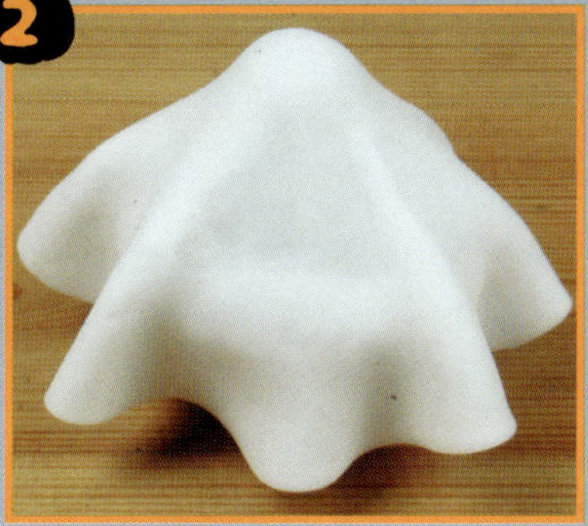

Pinch the center of the fondant circle to form a ghost shape.

3

Stick chocolate chip eyes and a mouth on, using a dab of icing from a tube.

4

Try forming a fondant ghost shape around a popsicle stick. Add chocolate chip eyes and a mouth.

5

Place your fondant ghost circles on top of the cupcakes.

TIP

To display your popsicle ghosts, you could push the sticks into a squash or pumpkin.

Cat Litter Treats

You Will Need

- 6 1/2 oz (185g) all-purpose flour
- 1 1/2 oz (40g) cocoa powder
- 1 teaspoon baking powder
- 7 tablespoons butter, cut into small pieces
- 6 oz (175g) sugar
- 1 extra large egg, beaten
- 1 teaspoon vanilla extract
- oil to grease the baking tray
- a package of oatmeal cookies

1

Adult Help

Ask an adult to heat the oven to 375°F (190°C). Rub a little oil over a large baking tray. Sift the flour, cocoa, and baking powder into a large bowl.

2

Using your fingertips, rub the butter pieces into the mixture until it has a texture like breadcrumbs.

3

Mix in the sugar. Add the beaten egg and vanilla. Mix with a spoon to make a soft dough.

4

Adult Help

Roll handfuls of dough into sausages or curl into spirals. Space them out on a greased baking tray. Bake for about 10 minutes until firm. Place them on a wire rack to cool.

5

While your cookies are cooling, make the litter tray. Crush the package of oatmeal cookies and spread the crumbs out onto a tray.

Finishing Touch

Arrange the poop on the litter tray. To make it super-gross, glaze the poop by brushing them with a little icing sugar mixed in warm water.

TIP

To make the cookie cat litter mess-free, put the cookies in a food bag. Then crush them with a rolling pin.

Snot Cocktail

You Will Need

- 1 package lime jello
- apple or pear juice
- lemonade
- sugar
- 1 cocktail glass

1

Make the lime jello following the package instructions. Chill it in the refrigerator until set.

2

Mix a glass of apple or pear juice with some lemonade. Chill the mixture in the refrigerator.

3

When the jello has set, break it up into small chunks using a whisk.

4

Tip some sugar onto a plate. Rub a wet finger around the rim of your cocktail glass. Press the rim into the sugar.

5

Spoon the jello into the cocktail glass. Top up with the apple juice mixture.

TIP

Make your snot cocktail even more gruesome. Skewer an eyeball from page 14 on a cocktail stick and pop it in the glass!

Hand Punch

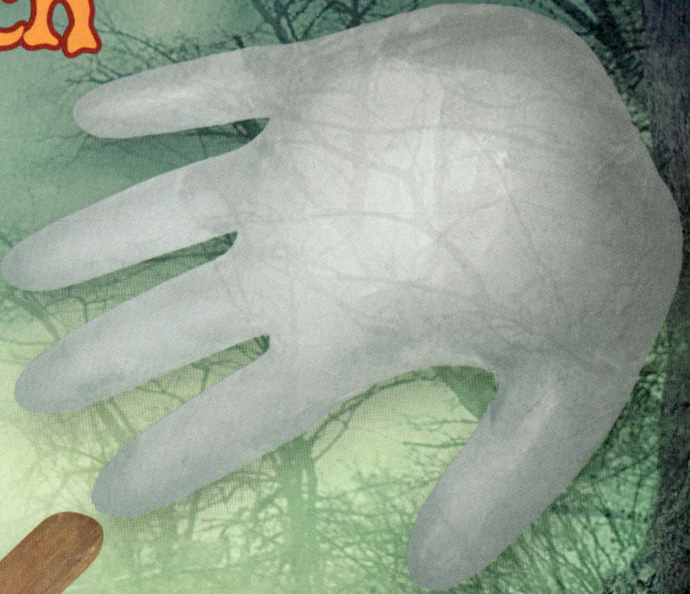

You Will Need

- blueberry, blackberry, or purple grape juice, chilled
- cherry or cranberry juice, chilled
- chilled sparkling water
- disposable gloves
- eyeballs from page 14

TIP

Wait until your guests arrive before you put the ice hands in the punch. They melt quite fast.

1

Rinse the disposable gloves and then fill each one with cold water.

2

Tie a knot in the top of each glove, like you would tie a balloon.

3

Freeze the gloves for several hours in the coldest part of the freezer.

4

While the hands are freezing, make the punch. Pour all the chilled juices into a large bowl.

5

Carefully peel the gloves from the ice hands. Put them back into the freezer until your guests arrive, then put them in the punch bowl.

6

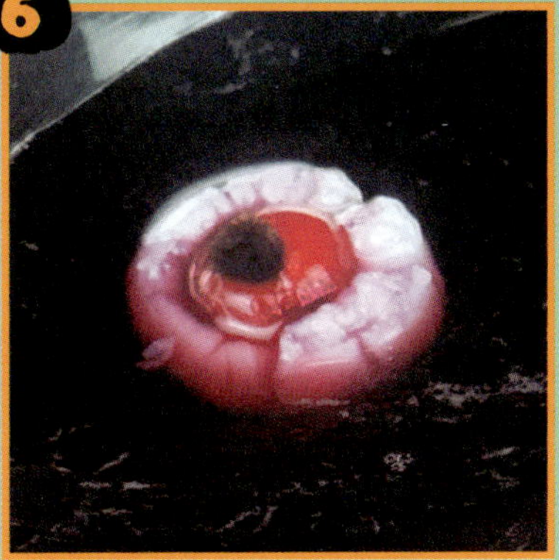

Add some eyeballs from page 14. Keep the punch in the refrigerator until you serve it.

Index